PERSPECTIVES
OF A
Life Lived

MARY HARRIS

PAGE PUBLISHING
Conneaut Lake, PA

First originally published by Page Publishing 2022

ISBN 979-8-88654-008-6 (pbk)
ISBN 979-8-88654-021-5 (digital)

Printed in the United States of America

To all of the courageous people, who
live in love, truth, and integrity.

Contents

Love and Relationships

Fathers and Daughters

March 1996

The first look at your eyes revealed an undying
source of energy, a connection that is like no other.

A father to his daughter.

Growing, playing, sharing memorable times
that would always be cherished.

This is a father and his daughter.

A female version of what and who he once was,
the features, personality, and behavior are uncanny.

A daughter to her father.

The protector, always concerned
and filled with advice,
just wanting the best for her.

For they are fathers and daughters.

Lost Love

Reaching, reaching, reaching,
Yes, I'm trying to reach out to you, baby!

Dreaming, dreaming, dreaming,
Just constantly dreaming about you!

Needing, needing, needing,
Needing every drop of your good loving!

But we can't connect, sorry!

For Now

• •

February 1995

I have chosen to accept us as we are,

to love you through it all.

Yet sometimes I try to find the strength
to let go!

I cannot!

So I have become accustomed to our
relationship as it is…

for now!

You Can't Relate

March 1, 1995

Sometimes when we converse,
I feel you're not there…

Maybe communication is down, or
you just don't care…

Life is too very brief for you not to hear me,
comprehend, and be here.

Free Spirit

My niece Rhonda visited me in
New York from Atlanta.

March 6, 2020

Up in the air you flew, coming to New York,
Totally blistered, for in a bar in
Atlanta, you popped a cork!

Not a care in the world, you
were coming to celebrate
the Fourth of July.
Since someone was picking you
up from the airport, you
had no need to fear or to cry!

The agenda was to celebrate but
also to look people up.
You arrived, toasted and looking for another cup!

From the subway with the family, you
disappeared to move around,
meeting old friends in Brooklyn
and in some other town!

Then you stayed out all night, just having great fun.
The final morning, you were gone and said,
"Oh, I just went for a run!"

After all, you're a free spirit who rises
and disappears like the sun!

Bingo

December 11, 2019

Bunnie, Bunnie, full of honey,
And you've won all the bingo money.
Whether it's raining or bright and sunny,
The jokes you tell at the table are always funny.

Sometimes people sit with you out of curiosity.
They've observed you from afar and
measured your generosity.

Trusting your wisdom as a retired educator.
Now they need advice, so you're a
counselor and moderator.

Respect from the status quo is all relevant
As your arrivals are seen as prevalent.

Forgiving Our Fathers

May 4, 1992

All during the week, you worked very hard…
Until it was Friday, when you became a drunkard.

Your personality changed and was so overwhelming.
Like Dr. Jekyll and Mr. Hyde,
it was so condemning.

I ran out to a neighbor to call the cops.
You had just grabbed our mother, and I wondered
what could happen if this man never stops.

Now the police have arrived on the scene.
Suddenly the excitement makes
me let out a loud scream.

The devastation you caused is still in my heart.
Now, today, you are born again, and it's hard for me
to keep it apart.

I Cried for You Today

To my husband, Travis

October 8, 2008

I cried for you today.
For all your efforts, I pray that God will open his
Floodgates of heaven and let it rain,
Especially since I feel your pain.

For ten years, you've worked in God's vineyard
To upkeep all of the Lord's standards.

Now the sheep have gone astray.
Through the hard times, they have lost their way.

But hold your head up high.
God may have new work, for it is written across
his sky.
I can do all things through Christ,
who strengthens me.
Oh Lord, my God, hear my plea!

I Didn't Know

Remembering Dad—Wesley Gilliard Jr.

January 12, 2018

I didn't know the month we spent together would be
our last major visit…
Here I was in New York, with time to reminisce
after a winter blizzard.
My sister and I had plans for a huge ninetieth
birthday bash.
We never thought that time would never become
a reality and be slashed…
I didn't know we were going to have to plan your
funeral four months later.
Oh, how we thought the doctors' prognosis were
wrong and that they were our haters.
For only God could say when
someone's time was up,
yet we eventually faced reality.
Each day, you grew weaker and were
losing your mortality.
Now every night I sob because you are no
longer among us living here.
So I comfort myself with the amazement of how
much I sincerely cared.
I didn't know I would miss you so much
and loved you more than I feared!

We Gathered Together

· ·

January 12, 2018

On a calm, chilly, calculated morning,
I rose, remembering the reality at hand.
Everyone was meeting at Dad's house to
travel in the family cars to the church.

After breakfast, I broke down, bellowing in blissful
sorrow. Nevertheless, I vacuumed, vanishing dust
from the varnish, and decorated
the end table with a vase.

Now I place a crystal fruit bowl with countless
mandarins in the center of the dining room table—
an inviting gesture as we gather there together.

Some of my siblings sounded surprised as they shouted,
"This is a cozy farmhouse!" For
dad was single and lived
a serene life yet simple.

Then I placed water bottles on a tray, walked around,
and waited for a while. For we
were gathered together, and
dad's recliner only held his suit
and Bible to symbolize him
posthumous.

At the church we sat, sad, sincere, and
secure. Only by one another's
soul's satisfaction for now were we
gathered together, alas,
by the love our father had for each of us.

Immaculate Patience

Dedicated to my dad—Wesley Gilliard Jr.

March 2, 2018

You had immaculate patience for your art.
We admired your work from the start.

Your imagination and concentration
could not be matched.
How you measured precisely even
down to the last stitch and catch.

The patience you demonstrated
was apparent in your eyes.
So everyone requested your work
for the beauty, not the size.

The enthusiasm for the use of pristine
quality fabrics was admired by many.
That's how you came highly recommended
and desired by plenty.

Your hands worked magic on designing drapes.
Watching you put special emphasis
by developing unique crepes.

You provided for all of your
customers a special touch.
Even made a room's decor pop with
a wonderfully placed hutch.

The imported materials you used to
design window shades and matching
headboards, created delightful rooms
in everyone's humble abodes.

People Destroying Other People

August 3, 1996

Deeply rooted, emotionally involved.
Serious and devoted…

Caring, caring, caring,
Waiting, waiting, waiting…

Disappointed and depressed.
Promises and chances…

Hurt and pain.
Anger and pain,
Pain and pain.
Pain and pain.

Chances and more broken promises.
Unparalleled relationships.
The giving and not receiving.
Total unfair treatment.
Vanished trust.
Actions versus reactions.

This is how people destroy other people.

I Cried Inside

Just looking at you, I see your heart is broken.
You have worked so hard and
been faithful, but nothing
Seems to be working.

Yet you never complain.
But I can feel your pain.

So I cried inside for you today.
Yes, I cried inside for you today.

I asked the Lord to be merciful and give you vision.
For I know you work to fulfill his glorious mission.

Just keep the faith, pray, and stand some more,
For the Lord is our battle axe and will restore.

Because I love you, I cried inside for you today.
Yes, I cried inside for you today.

Although weeping endureth for a night,
I cried inside for you today.
Oh, I cried inside for you today.

So I will pray for you and cry inside anyway.

A Mother's Love

To myself, with love!

May 1990

Mother, you have shown me the first
love I've ever had.

Whenever I see your smile, it makes me glad.
Never judging me but just loving me, letting
me know there is nothing to fear.

The calmness of your spirit radiates
throughout our home.

From the flower arrangements throughout our house
to that time and place where you
gently stroked our hair and
styled it uniquely with a comb.

Oh, your magical touch gives an
individual hairdo and style.

Then we admire the way you cut
dad's nails and keep it
well groomed with a file.

Mother, your love inspires and abounds.

It's felt in every way, and each day it astounds.

If You Take Me Back

July 1991

I'll give you more love than before,
Much, much more than you can endure,
If you take me back.

You used to reach out to me,
But I used to have somewhere else to be.
Now I promise you will see a big change in me
If you take me back.

Each night and day I pray
That God will show me the way
To convince you to let me stay
But only
If you take me back.

Communication Block

July 13, 1995

I can't reach you! There was nobody
home. I phoned and spoke
to a stranger several times. But there
was a communication block.

Where were you? Well, where are
you now? Do you understand
what I just said?

Yes, I know you love me, but
your actions do not exist!

I need you to be there for me, to do things with me.

No, I don't want to scratch your back!
Again, you did not hear me!

Mother's Wit

Dedicated to my mother—Wilhelmina J. Gilliard

July 27, 1995

Self-educated and always with an opinion.
Wise, mild-mannered, and caring.
Filled with joy and understanding.
Mother has a wit about her.

Quiet, clear-minded, and direct, she
welcomes the world as it is,
Allowing room for mistakes but
Still there to comfort all who are burdened.

Foreseeing, estimating, and calculating, almost
precise, a genius in her own rite.

Mother has good wits!

Sparing Pain

July 27, 1995

Quiet, no one needs to know.
We both understand what is happening
between us.

That illegal love,
oh, what a sin, but how good it feels.
A relief when the world is unkind!
Soothing over the rough areas of a
bruised heart.

But quiet, no one needs to know.
For there are innocent people who
might get hurt!

So we must spare pain at all cost!

Every Bit of You

October 24, 1995

Thinking about you often and just visualizing
the way you look! All the things about you
that just turn me on…

Your shy smile, it makes it happen to me each time!
I get completely gassed up and steamed.
Those eyes, they look right through me. You put
me under a spell! I am yours forever…

The way you walk, cool and smooth, just so
certain about yourself. So confident! And you
should be too…

I think you are wonderful!

Every bit of you!

You Look Good

August 1991

There you were, standing there. I
wanted to approach you, but I
Wouldn't dare. When I got the nerve to
do so, I wondered if you would tell
Me to go. But you just looked at me
and smiled. Your eyes were saying
To me, "You look good."

All I could do was stand there and stare.
I couldn't believe you still cared.
All I could say to myself was, "You look good."

Yes, I regret the day I let you go. But
forever I want you to know that
I'm happy your life is going smoothly.
You now have found another
To share your life with. I'm glad
you made her your wife.

I just want to say, "You look good."

The Power of Reciprocating

<hr>

July 9, 2019

When someone attends your party, remember to
return the favor.
It is considered hearty.
For if you don't, you will be called a farty!

Even if you can't stay, appearance matters
in every way.
Show that you care and would love to convey
and play.

Sometimes you're busy and might run late.
It's all right. Just get started and proceed before
all the guests leave and walk out of the gate!

It's always important to treasure others, smile,
and reciprocate!

The Princes of Pennsylvania

May 13, 2019

Four grandsons moved from the
Rockaways in New York
to the Poconos in Pennsylvania,
So we geared up to visit them, going through all
the traffic mania…

Up and down the mountains and
through the valley's low
we would go

Just to see our princes of Pennsylvania!

My, how they had grown, and
very proper they did speak.
We wondered and pondered about
how much of their own
culture they would keep.

For now, they were the princes of Pennsylvania.

They were the best behaved
children in Florida's airport,
Waiting patiently for us to instruct
them on what to do next. We
had a great rapport.

Well-mannered are the princes of Pennsylvania!

Bright smiles and filled with hope and dreams are
the princes of Pennsylvania!

Memorials

Remembering Angie

May 6, 2020

The look on your face as we walked
through the airport was astonishing.
As you walked us all through security first
made you glow, filled with life and promise.

A sense of pride gave you a boost of energy
to lead us first unto the plane.
You then closed up your walker and
didn't even need a cane.

Everyone was at your beck and call.
We were happy because you were happy
and just didn't want to see you fall.

Everywhere we went in Florida, we were always first
With you championing upfront,
ahead of the longest
lines, which were the worst.

How lucky we felt in Universal
Studios at all of the rides.
All of us followed you as the
attendant instructed you
to come in through the express side.

Seeing you climb into the hammock on the Fourth
of July was a sight to see.
As you watched everyone eat and
dance, you were filled with glee.

These are the final memories I have of you.
The loud laugh and twinkle in your
eyes, I won't forget those too.

An Ode to Jacobi (Cobi) Johnson

April 6, 2019

That smile was brilliant and bright,
Shining down on all of us, sitting in your sight.

When you arrived in the evenings, home from work,
we waited patiently, for you always
had a joke and a smirk.

Your tall stature commanded attention,
and of that we felt so proud.
You walked in, standing erect, and never acted loud.

Those tiny, twinkling eyes made
us feel assured and calm.
You were never bringing home any trouble,
so we never felt a need to be alarmed.

Shock and shook we were about
the news that you're gone.
Our thoughts are wandering rapidly
because there is a part of us
that feel so alone.

Now we pray and ask God for serenity,
Deep down, anxious to why this had to be…

You left us too soon and quickly,
So we cried uncontrollably and felt sickly.

Only the divine Savior can fix this hurt.
With time and life's experiences, it will all work.

Relax, our souls to live on and conquer for sure.
Remember the moments you gave us and how
it was everything and more.

-My grandnephew will always remain in our hearts.
Gone too soon! We love you!

Farewell, See You One Day

From Wesley Gilliard, aka Junior

To my friends and family far and near,
On earth I loved you all so dear
And tried to express how much I cared,
But now I'm caught up with the Master…
The voices sounded so familiar
as well as the laughter.
There I saw my son, mother, father,
sister, and three brothers.

They all astounded me with the
smiles on their faces and said,
"Welcome home! Good to see
you, you are not alone!"
So I'll see you one day and greet
you with the same love.
Until then, rest assured I'll watch
over you from above.

Written with love, your daughter, Bunnie

An Ode to J. C.

August 1996

J. C. was like a father-in-law to me.

J. C., as many of us so affectionately
called him, liked living life.
I can recall the many stories he's
shared with me about his
boyhood in Rockaway, New York.

Some of the stories, for instance,
were about Rockaway being a
swamp-landfill and the movie stars
living and vacationing in
Rockaway Beach's bungalows.

What amazed me most about J. C.'s
boyhood was that his best friend
at P. S. 42 was White, and this was in the
1920s! He loved all people, was full
of fun, and made everyone laugh.
That's what I'll miss most.

The twinkle in his eyes when he smiled
brightened the spirit in my soul.
I feel that he is smiling down on us at
this moment and wants us to live
life and be happy. I will always
remember the fun person he was.

An Ode to Songbird

Dedicated to the memory of my
mother-in-law, Edna Harris

February 2018

Singing for the children at 105 school,
Reminding them that they are never to be a fool.

A raging voice singing, "If I can help
somebody," at a going-home
service in the church,
Standing in front of the congregation
was the songbird's perch.

People stood immediately, getting to their feet,
Testifying, shouting, and screaming,
"Jesus!" as they cried for her
to sing again, so she made everyone
happy with a repeat.

Although she's gone on to live with
Jesus in heaven and home,
You've always reminded us in song
that we are never alone!

The Transition

Written upon hearing of a female's death

June 15, 2017

I have transitioned into the spiritual world,
Leaving you to cherish all the memories of when
I was a girl.

Yes, I saw the light…
Yes, I took the flight.

I saw my mother's smile and my father's face.
That's how I knew I was in the right place.

So I hope to see you there
With all the relatives that care.

Until then, goodbye,
And please don't cry.

For I will be watching you daily from on high.

Gone Too Soon

. . . .

An Ode to Juanita Grayson,
Middle School 226 Dean

April 27, 2013

You're an angel with wings
because you were gone too soon...
Now you're looking down at us,
right next to our guardian at night, the moon.
Remembering your wide, confident smile
when you won at hearings and declared the victory
as though they were major trials...
Seeing you monitor and sit, in-charge
of the students during
detention,
Knowing that you really only showed
them love by giving out
advice and props, which was
really a compensation...
The things you did for them may
never all be truly known,
But they will remember your hallway
presence and how they
were shook then scattered to their
hiding places, only to be
discovered by you where they had flown...

So as we walk the corridors of this
school until the end of June,
Your protective spirit's presence will give
us hope for our future although
you are gone too soon.

(Well done, thou good and faithful servant. May
your soul rest in eternal peace with the Almighty.)

Welcome Home

July 27, 2018

Welcome home
Welcome home
We've been waiting for you
So welcome home

Welcome home
The pearly gates are open wide
So welcome home

Welcome home
Welcome home
You will live in peace for all eternity

So welcome home

Uncle Willie,
Gone to Glory

January 23, 2020

I can recall the summer days spent on the farm.
Everything was serene and quiet, with no alarm.
The green trees swayed in the warm wind and
had a tranquilizing charm.

Uncle Willie could be seen in the fertile field on
the horizon, far away
While us children played on the porch our regular
games of jacks and cards until the sun went down.

It's where we would stay.
School had just let out. So it was to the country
we went at the end of each May.

Some days were spent picking
watermelon, tomatoes,
and beans with fields of corn,
Hauling it to the markets by pickup
truck and horse and wagon
very early in the morn.

Contemplating each year the best crops to grow,
Uncle Willie focused on what to
grow and what will sell while
analyzing the market's flow.

Responsible for at least three families' farmsteads,
He listened and cared for all the elders' foresights
as well as their meds.

So much on his shoulders for years in and out.
With a smile on his face, never
burdened, never even a pout.

Always relying on God to be his saving grace,
Never worrying or giving up, for
the farm was his main place.

Understanding we are on this
earth but for a short time.
Knowing his children would carry on
the work made him feel sublime.

Uncle Willie has now run a long
course and went on to glory,
With all his offspring, family, and friends
and church left to tell his story.

An Ode to Gerri

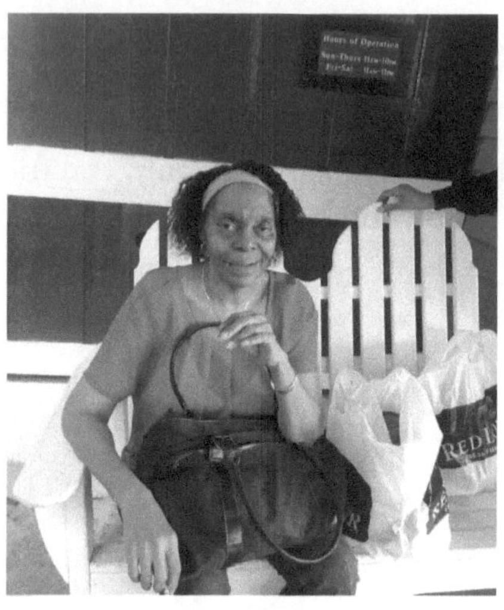

March 15, 2020

You lived a life so filled with hope
As you planned with purpose to help you cope.

Life's situations didn't always deal you an easy hand.
Still, you championed on the best you can.

Sometimes it appeared that
everything was going wrong!
You never gave up and just remained strong.

Understanding that God had a plan for you.

Working and saving was your mantra and
and all that you could do.

Raising your sons was the love of your life.
Just seeing them grow and smile
removed all your strife.

Traveling with your husband, mother,
and sisters was a highlight.
Although your health kept failing,
you made it, in hindsight.

So we will treasure the holidays spent at your house,
How you danced and hosted
along with your spouse.

You have moved on to our family's
mansion in the sky.
We ask that the Lord and ancestors
love you and won't
ever ask God why.

Godspeed, sis, we'll see you again.
Well done, thou good and faithful servant.
I will see you in my thoughts and dreams.
I love you.

Uncle Willie

January 1, 2020

A great patriarch of our family
has gone home to God.
Uncle Harry made a joke and
smiled wide as Uncle Willie
walked through the pearly gates.
He said, "Welcome home,
big brother, you old geezer!" My
dad, Junior, cried and ran to
greet him with a big hug. They had
gotten very close in those
last few years and adored one another
respectfully. As the three
brothers entered the family's white
mansion there in the sky, they were
greeted by many others who dwelled
there. There his mother, father, sister,
and two more brothers stood with joy as
they entered. My brother, nephews,
and nieces and some infants were there as
well. Several great-great-grandparents
and family members looked on in awe!
Uncle Willie's son James and
Aunt Lee, his wife, moved forward with
opened arms of love and embraced him.

For God's promises are true, and Jesus
went to prepare this place. Now they
are reaping the heavenly glories there with
him. My dad is playing his guitar
again and using the finger he lost in his
twenties. Grandma, Aunt Lee, and Aunt
Bertha Lee are preparing desserts for all to
enjoy at the homecoming celebration.
The homemade biscuits are placed in the
cookie jar daily. Fresh string beans, greens,
tomatoes, and squash as well as meats and all the
foods from the farm are stored in the smokehouse.

The family lovingly miss all of you, and we
know you came for Uncle Willie. It was
his time to come and live in our heavenly
home. We pray to arrive there one day
and enjoy your presence again. For we
love you, but God loves you best!

God's Grace

A Sense of Being

May 1, 2020

Knowing where you come from is so awesome.
How your forefathers struggled and won invokes
character and allows one to blossom.

Hearing early the words "You
come from good people"
is so valuable and rewarding, as
your family church's steeple.

It rises above everything else you stand for.
Upon it, some decisions are made
and measured like the law.

Giving you structure for dreams and hope.
Also the courage to try and allow
yourself to be ambitious
and the ability to cope.

Staying strong in stature
with morals to live a clean and caring life
is what's displayed and captured.

A sense of being is important to
determine your future plans,
Evaluating the objectives and placement of people,
places, and other demands.

Step Back

• •

April 26, 2019

When times come in that we don't understand,
We step back and obey your words, oh Lord.

When you call our loved ones home, dear Lord,
We step back and bow our heads, my God.

So I feel alone, oh Lord,
I step back.

And the comforter soothes me,
and I thank you, Lord.
Oh, just step back.

Even when troubles come, oh Lord,
We step back. Yes, we step back.

Nothing Else Matters

January 2000

When I sit quietly, I feel your spirit.
It consumes the best of me, and my
soul rejoices.

Nothing else matters to me. Your
grace is upon my soul.

So nothing else matters to me.

I live with thee each day. I desire your
guidance. So I seek your face. Then
you comfort me all the way.

Now nothing else matters to me. Your
grace is upon my soul.

So nothing else matters to me. For I
give thee all of my thanks!

The Miracle Maker

1993

God performed a miracle in my life.
He made a way when there was no way
to be made.

He asked me to trust him and to keep the
faith. Soon I found myself in unbelievable
positions. How grateful I felt!

"Why me, oh Lord?" I asked, and his spirit
replied, "Why not you, my child? For you have
been faithful and obedient, and I love you."

Lord, I love you because you are a miracle maker.
For only you could have possibly
kept and brought me
to where I am today!

I've Got to Tell It

1993

I've got to tell it! About the Graces
of God and how he
came into my life one day and turned me around.

He saw that I was troubled and
took my burdens away.
Then he told me, "There is no
need to worry or go astray."

He lifted me up and gave me glory
through his love. How
sweet it has been since Jesus found me!

Now I'm happy and worry-free!

Hey, God

August 5, 2019

Hey, God, I love you…
When I look upon my life and
see all the miracles you've done,
I can continue on with a smile and have fun.

Hey, God, I love you…
Seeing generations of my life
rise from the dust,
it lets me know you will never forget.
You will never forget us.

Hey, God, I love you…
Even when the storms sometimes
bring me down,
you keep my spirit inspired.
Hallelujah! I can go on and
keep you above all I have admired.
For you have never let me down!

Praise Him

November 2, 2003

Praise Jesus and my Father above,
Praise him…
Thou who sits on high and looks down low,
Praise him…
For I come to worship our Lord and Savior,
Praise him…
As I walk the streets, I will
Praise him…
When I am with my family and friends, we will
Praise him…
The times my adversaries attack
me, I will remember to
Praise him…
My life will be all right, and I am so
blessed for the knowledge to
Praise him.

The Dignified Sanctified

July 13, 1995

Just look at them! Praising the Lord
In front of the church.

You have to look because you certainly can't
Hear or feel the Spirit working within them.

They are the dignified sanctified!
Their praising is silent, personal,
And always held within.

Maybe they feel that they would
wrinkle their clothes,
People would watch them, or they will become
Uncontrollable, praising the Lord.

For they are the dignified sanctified.

The Devil-Angel Syndrome

* * *

July 13, 1995

Oh, my sister, what is the matter?
You are having a deeply rooted problem!

Your stare tells of an unbearable jealousy.
While you work, seating all the worshippers,
Your adversary walks through the door.

Yes, you want what she has and perhaps to be her.
But pray and give it to God to
help you from within.
For right now, your mind is scheming. Don't do it!

Find yourself fast!

The Sweet Blood of Jesus

April 1995

Oh, the price!

Oh, the sacrifice!

Oh, the journey and pain!

Oh, the crucifix!

It bears my Jesus…

The dripping of the blood!

Oh, it replenished my soul,

When the soil receives his sweet
Blood for a new life!

Stomp Out the Devil

February 15, 2009

It seems my life is spiraling downhill.
A voice from God said, "Child, don't worry,
just say I will…
Stomp, stomp, stomp, stomp, out the devil,
Stomp, stomp, stomp, stomp, out the devil."
My world was built with prayer and inspiration,
for Jesus was my avid consternation. He said…
"Stomp, stomp, stomp, stomp, out the devil,
Stomp, stomp, stomp, stomp, out the devil"
Now I can plan each day to
prosper and build higher,
for with you, I know the devil is a liar. So I'll just…
Stomp, stomp, stomp, stomp, out the devil,
Stomp, stomp, stomp, stomp, out the devil.

The Keepers

January 24, 1991

Humans are not the most
civilized creatures beneath
God's sun.

Look at the massive destruction
they have done…

Sometimes I feel another species
could have managed better.

At least all of creation would have
been preserved, and everything
would matter.

Creation

1991

Though God created the world in seven days

It is man's duty to make sure that it stays

So many are corrupt and blind

What will ever become of mankind?

I pray that a revelation will come

That eventually we can live as one
under God's sun,

To be patient with one another
and love one another as according to the Father.

Praise My Lord

January 27, 1992, 1:00 a.m.

Praise my Lord in the days
of sorrow

Praise my Lord in the days
of joy

For we don't know what will
come with tomorrow

But praise Him!
Praise my Lord!
Praise Him!
Praise Him!

Praise my Lord!

Perspectives

Black-Girl Power

April 25, 2020

A genius can take nothing and
make it into something.
Just with thought, she can make someone else's
disregarded items sing!

Frills with a stamp on it—it becomes fancy,
expensive looking, not like it was a
knock-off bought from Delancey Street.

A problem can spark a dream,
especially when life gets rough,
makes you desperate, and sends you to extremes.

Each day brings a bright idea,

leading to planning step by step
with no emotional care.

It's not a want but a must.
Leaving all tender feelings aside,
even those deep passions are derived from lust.

This is a Black girl's power.
No season or weather outside can stop her,
not even a downpour or shower.

The Students

May 13, 2019

The student is always wide-eyed and eager to learn,
Entering the classroom each day,
doing their diligence to get
The highest mark earned.

Staying competitive and applying
their skills to be worthy,
Accordingly, always conducive,
Never daydreaming, nonattentive, and illusive…

Reaching their goals and objectives daily
to show themselves approved,
Never interruptive and negative, causing
themselves to be removed…

But proud and knowledgeable,
Only remaining respectable…

With an aim to become a future
leader, this is undeniable!

Fall Is...

······································

September 1996

Fall is a chilly season.
It comes right after the summer.
It lasts until December.
Many things happen in the fall.
Birds migrate south, and many animals hibernate.
We must wear jackets in the fall.
The holidays during the fall are
Labor Day, Rosh Hashanah,
Yom Kippur, Columbus Day, Halloween,
Election Day, Veterans Day,
and, of course, Thanksgiving.
As Americans, most of us celebrate
all or some of them.
The best part of the season is the farmers'
harvest; squirrels gathering nuts;
and enjoying the foliage as the leaves
turn red, orange, yellow, and brown.

Do You Even Know?

October 25, 2019

Do you even know how it all went down?
No, you were too busy flaunting and wearing
your self-proclaimed crown.

How many students were in uproar in protest,
ready to make you feel the pain?
No, but I am sure you celebrated with a random or
someone else's spouse, drinking champagne.

They grew tired of the nonsense and
were ready to put you down.
But I said with respect, "No! I have got
this," willing to take the legal ground.

But the city is so corrupt! Anything out
of the norm, they view as far-fetched
and abrupt. They flip it back your way!
Sending abusive leaders was the ticket of the day.
Becoming a whistleblower, revealing
the shenanigans of how the
push-outs and hits was the new play!

Blatant disrespect and taunting, eager for a reaction.
No, don't do it! They will call you
insubordinate and irate.
Don't give them the satisfaction!

California State of Mind

October 15, 2019

Relaxing and always warm is the California breeze…
Awakening to a calm morning,
picking ripened oranges
from the backyard to prepare fresh
juice with a little squeeze.

Cherishing the moments I spend
with my sister and her family,
It's sad others can't be here, we are
so embroiled in a calamity.

We must be cognizant about how life fleets…
Have we not learned how to love and
the importance of a greeting?

I pray God will restore our family to forgive
Unless our existence will be in vain and not how our
forefathers intended us to live!

Why can't we all be here together, making amends?
Life does not promise tomorrow…
Now we should have learned
lessons from all the sorrows.

It's so beautiful here. How could you not be happy?
Look at one another and be kind…
Just relish in the California state of mind!

A Las Vegas State of Mind

September 2019

It's dawn, and the sun is coming over the mountains
in the desert's horizon.

Natives are up early, going to work in the casinos,
While others starting their day are rising.

Take a day tour to the nearby Hoover Dam or the
Grand Canyon.

Visit the museums and many
shops. Go to the Indian
Reservation for some cultural experiences.

A bustling oasis in the desert,
always a happy atmosphere.
See dusk as the bright, colorful night-
lights put on a show. Stroll the strip
slowly after a hearty meal.

Smiles on everyone's faces, fun was surely had by all!
People hate to go home.
After another year passes, again they will arrive with
family, friends, or even alone.

An Ode to Rockaway, New York

March 1, 2018

Waves wandering and whaling on the wide shores.
Many shells washed in sequentially according to size
and in scores.
The foam famously refreshing the
sands, making them inviting.
People patiently walk politely, peering
at their footprints, and
that's always exciting.
See young ones splish and splash as
they simultaneously swim.
Parents spot and recognize their
heads above the water's rim.
Some concession stands' food
smell, soar, and succeed,
alluring customers while many stood,
situated in a line, peering up
at a succulent menu to read.
Players on the paddleball court
plunge at a small rubber ball,
pitting petty comments like, "Oh," "Yes,"
"Indeed," and "Shut out. I call."
Bikers based their pace briskly, basking in the air,
being aware to brake for beachgoers with care.

DJs playing melodic, motivating music in the park,
making everyone dance with movement,
hustling and breaking
until it's dark.
Rockaway is a particular and
peculiar place for everyone,
whether you are rich or poor, there
is always a way to have fun!

Filling a Void

January 15, 1996

After realizing that a mother's
love couldn't fill the void,

I became embarrassed and seriously annoyed.

Going through the motions was quite a thrill,

Getting into jams and telling lies against my will,

So much to do with so little time,

Trying to come back to reality
and claim what was mine,

Thanking God for bringing me safely through,

I've learned that all of the love you
need is already inside you.

An Era of Deflection

December 7, 2019

The art of deflection often changes the direction
of which way the judge will go.
People of power think they rule,
getting funds off the books and
claiming they will use it
for the good of the people.
Yet politically, it's never known
where the money has gone.
Students, teachers, and neighborhoods still suffer!
They have been blinded by the nonprofit
programs used to front and buffer.
But it's only a facade! So no one
would ask questions and put up
a guard. The students are called
disadvantaged and poor. Don't worry
about it. They will never make the score!
Teachers shout, "Stop taking
away from the downtrodden. Quit deflecting.
To us, they will never be forgotten!"

Gay Paris

December 22, 2019

Reflecting on a visit to Paris
makes me feel shy and embarrassed

Of how joyful I feel.
Being in Paris at fifty was such a steal.

We walked the streets, making
sounds of awe and oh!

The ancient-looking buildings and the scenery
made us feel full and free.

Views of people dancing along the river Seine
made us jump with glee and feel so fine.

I will forever have gay Paris on my mind!

Hawaiian Dreams

December 11, 2019

With a view overlooking the Pacific
Ocean and the Sugar Loaf volcano,
I feel mesmerized.
People moved around the beaches
and zoo as though they
have been hypnotized.

As we walked among others on the street,
our eyes meet and glowingly greet.

There are no bad days in Honolulu.
You feel free to stroll even without a pair of shoes.

Oh, the colors of the flowers make you stare
As though they will grant you
unknown powers, as if they care.

I am rejuvenated and happy.
My laughs and smiles, for no
necessary reasons, are so sappy.

The music at the gatherings are
so deep with feelings.
People dance and prance under the
sky—an unlimited ceiling.

We all agree to visit again soon
to dance and shout under the moon.

Florida's Rays

December 22, 2019

Sunshine shocked my soul,
Glowing and glazing like pure gold.

Everyone evolving endlessly,
Visiting venturously all the venues,

Advertised amenities and adventures.

The rays radiating and rotating along the roads with
rippling effects.

Carolina Courtesy

December 22, 2019

Carolina courtesy is contagious.
Smiling faces are a simple sample of a situation
surrounding the sunshine each day while strolling
the stone squares on the sidewalks.

The air smells of shellfish from the high tides
smothering the shores and sizzling in the air.
The solemnness and calmness are easy, always
energizing the silence but are
tranquilizing, as seagulls
sing while night draws near.

Hat Personality

April 9, 1992

A hat talks about the person who wears it.
It often tells what type of mood the person's in.

A person can wear a wide-brimmed
hat to express himself
feeling calm and collected—very sure of himself!

Some people wear tall, floppy hats
when they feel cool and
just want to hang out, hats like
the "LL Cool J" style.

People wear fluffy fur hats if they
have money and some
prestige. These hats put them in
the spending mood. They
normally would buy something
expensive from a designer
like Gucci or Fendi or from a store
like Bloomingdale's, Tiffany,
Or Saks Fifth Avenue.

Yes! A hat tells it all.

Desire

. . . .

All humans have desire.
Some desire to be rich…

Some have a desire for food,
especially those who are overweight…

Some people have desires for materialistic things
like sports cars, designer clothing,
and traveling abroad…

Some people have desires for
simple things in life like
a family, a home, and an education…

Yet some people just desire to be healthy and alive.

Red-Eyed Monday

So I didn't get much sleep last
night. First, the baby came
with us then poked his feet in my
stomach and chest all night!

Now my spouse snored enough to
awaken the dead. Each time I
coaxed him into turning over, the sound
became louder and had a whistle
at the end!

Suddenly the cat jumped on top of
me. Maybe she wanted to play
or eat. So I got up, played with her,
and gave her something to eat!

Surprisingly, it was time to get ready
for work. I peered in the mirror at
my face. I reached for makeup and Visine!

Well, it's another red-eyed Monday
for me—how special!

When Life Fleets

August 8, 2019

Our times together, when we shared,
it was obvious how much we cared.

Your smile is meshed into my brain.
I recall it vividly as I wipe away the tears,
for the salt always leaves a stain.

The brightness of your complexion
reveals a dreamy reflection,

as though I was staring at you, from a watery pool.
It kept me calm, relaxed, and cool.

Now you're leaving me! I fear we
will never get it back.
So life fleets, and I feel like a rugged,
broken-down old shack!

America in Turmoil

September 18, 2019

What happened to the land of the
free and the home of the brave?
For decades now, it seems as though
all we did is dig graves!

I don't know why all of a sudden
we need gun control.
Gone are most of the days when we
had to run from the slave patrol.

Kids are afraid in their classrooms daily.
Just studying and doing homework
was a job accomplished barely.
Once never being afraid to walk
to school or get shot rarely!

People just seem more angry and on edge,
similar to a hungry beast let out of its cage.
No one casually speaks to one another
for fear of unwarranted rage.

They suspect one another of using an alternative
motive when greetings have become a labor.
So now no one bothers to care and can't
take a chance to love thy neighbor!

It mostly does not exist anymore!
In many cases, no one's ever been
inside another's door.

People just don't have morals
and one another's backs.
However, in anger, they are quick to join the attack.

There is so much displaced,
unnecessary anger on our soil.
It's hard to trust anyone, and that's
why America is in turmoil!

The Little Gray Cat

Dedicated to all the furrow cats in Long Island,
New York, and those who care for them

April 26, 2017

I saw a little cat.
In my backyard, near the vegetable garden, she sat.
She was watching the birds in the trees.
Then I noticed her near the flowers by
the garage, peering at the bees.
So I went into the yard to say hello.
Her eyes became large and started to glow.

To calm her, I said, "Here, kitty, kitty."
She walked over to me slowly and a bit witty.
I stroke her gray fur from her head to tail.
We both appeared calm, and our
first meeting didn't fail.
Now each day I put food and water
out for her on the patio.
The little gray cat comes early to make a score.
I leave a tennis ball as a toy.
She rolls and taps it continuously.
Showing it brings such a joy.
The little gray cat has become my loyal friend.
We have so much fun together.
I hope it will never end.

If I Could Live Again

June 13, 2004

Looking at you makes me wonder
about what my life would be like
if I could live again…
Seeing your deep chocolate, so pure
and unstained, what if it was me?
But only if I could live again…
Hearing your indigenous speech, so
foreign and royal, now I wonder if
I would know the language of the motherland.
If only I could live again…
You are who I would have been
if it wasn't for that dammed middle passage…
You will always be who I should have
been, and maybe in another lifetime,
we will be one.
If we could live again…
I love you, my African kindred.

The Manipulator

February 9, 2019

Oh, the behavior, so contrite,
pretending to do what's right
although the adversary is out of sight.
The phone calls during the night mostly
started the mind fights.
Seeing yourself as a peacemaker, you're
really nothing but everyone's nemesis and
such a faker,
a connoisseur of conniving a situation and
placing it on display,
confiscating information and pretending not to
be conscience of all the elements and blown away…
You're just a mere manipulator of what everyone
has to say!

Jamaican Breezes

February 24, 2020

Warm winds blow
in waves of the Jamaican air. Wow!

Mesmerizing, mystically making magic
through the atmosphere. Oh man!

Relaxing the mind, rejuvenated
by the region's restored mountainside. Real!

Twisting, twirling roads,

a way to the top of the
tossing waterfalls! Tantalizing!

Falls filling streams
flowing over with funny
flaunting folks. Facts!

Just enjoying the breezes
of Jamaica while joking and
and feeling jolly and filled with joy. Jump! Jump!

Coronavirus Panic

March 30, 2020

People with money, are buying up everything,
while people without, had to learn how to wing it.
Others at home, cleaning, playing
games, and humming
out of boredom, they sing.

Some never coming out of doors for days,
just looking out of the window, at the
sunshine overcast with a haze.
Seeing the birds scattering, looking for food
through a virtual maze.

The cancellation of airplane flights to and fro.
No vacations now or soon. Who knows when we
can go?
Only living day by day, and going
along with the flow.

Sadly, funerals of the virus' victims are on hold.
As families worry and plan to prepare by viewing
companies, where caskets and burials are sold.
Anxious for the final preparations of their deceased
loved one, they are ready to roll.

Watching the news daily, only
tuning once in a while,
for updates only, and clear not
to interrupt the home's
atmosphere and style.
Trying to stay as normal as possible,
but driving only locally, not past a mile.

Oh Ye in High Places

. . . .

February 15, 2018

Having the authority and power
doesn't mean to exploit,
Oh ye in high places…
But treat people with fairness and
supportive compassion, or sacrifice
Your blessings, for God will not anoint,
Oh ye in high places…
Never be persuaded by others'
agenda to bring about ruin,
Oh ye in high places…
Just keep your eyes on the prize, remember
what you were originally pursuing,
Oh ye in high places…
Why would you want to be a devil's advocate?
Oh ye in high places…
Falsely discrediting and accusing others,
Oh ye in high places…
Stemmed in your jealousy, and
hurt possibly from youth,
Oh ye in high places…
Cold, calculating, your attacks on the subordinates,
Oh ye in high places…
Creating nonexistent scenarios to devalue your prey,
Oh ye in high places…

Always using nepotism and cronyism
to assist with your infamous,
Lowlife schemes,
Oh ye in high places…
Your life's all about being able to lie and connive,
Oh ye in high places…
So narcissistic and psychotic, hating to
see others gathered in camaraderie,
Oh ye in high places…
Disturbing the Americana persona,
bravely fought for,
Oh ye in high places…
Using the Machiavellian approach to divide
workers and conquer by starting rumors,
Oh ye in high places…
Getting caught up in other people's wars
because you joined the clique,
Oh ye in high places…
Keeping your status quo even if you
had to get on your knees—please!
Oh ye in high places…
Hey, you would have even sold your mother,
Oh ye in high places…
Framing person after person because
they would not sabotage another,
Oh ye in high places…
Pathetic and anxious, always needing to
be nominated for an award or be
In the Hall of Fame,
Oh ye in high places…

Forcing the unbrave and scared
to people to bow down,
Oh ye in high places…
Your discontent with life made you bitter
and lash out against successful,
Professional masters,
Oh ye in high places…
Giving credit to what was relevant
never occurred to you,
Oh ye in high places…
Just being on top and keeping your domination,
Oh ye in high places…
The sociopath you are is obvious and ever present,
Oh ye in high places.

Comatose

Sometimes while I am thinking,
I feel like I am asleep.
I go off into a state of shock.

So many disappointing situations,
I begin to feel as though they were
just bad nightmares.

But then I feel the cry inside
and know that they were very real.

The many mistakes and wrong
directions I took become so clear.

Still, I sit in a comatose stage
and wonder how to fix my life.

No Changes

July 13, 1995

They still sit around and gossip about us,
all the latest that the news shows said,

Judgmentally analyzing us as though they are
the persona of human perfection,

Always thinking that we are society's worst problem,
and the country would be farther along if we weren't
a part of it…

Listening,
listening to them day after day,
year after year, watching
their hatred build. Maybe they even
long for a definite solution
to this scar on their perception of a perfect society,

But they seem to pray to be
removed and not help those
people, not one bit…

For they are privileged and expect to
keep it that way. Never to share
the riches of this wonderful country with
others because their forefathers
taught and deemed it so!

Why can't they see that they are a part
of the problem? Because they
won't help bring change.

I Remember

February 4, 1993

I remember waiting up on Christmas
Eve for Santa Claus.
Although, Mom said that if he
caught us looking, he would
spit tobacco in our eyes.
I remember being afraid of the bogeyman.
In the pitch-black darkness of the night,
I remember placing my tooth under
my pillow for the tooth fairy
In order to get money for goodies the next day.
I remember walking through floods after a long rain.
I remember the beautiful rainbow
after a long rainstorm.
I remember my brothers and I trying
to reach the end of the rainbow
on our bikes to get the pot of gold.
I remember swimming in the muddy
creek at the back of the graveyard.
I remember scooping up tadpoles
from puddles in an empty jar.
I remember watching hundreds of baby
frogs jumping all over our yard.
I remember the first time I went into
the haunted house at Disney World
and how afraid I was.

I remember driving in traffic for the first
time and how other drivers were
speeding past me!
I remember the smell of fireworks at
the Fourth of July barbecues.
I remember how sad my family was
when my grandmother died.
I remember how special I felt when I
was honored as an educator at the
Waldorf Astoria.
I remember seeing a dead cat lying in the street.
I remember going to the ice cream
parlor after Sunday school.
I remember my mother's voice as she
sang lead in the church choir.
I remember the trips each summer and
picking fresh vegetables on my
uncle's farm.
I remember riding a horse for the first time.
I remember how afraid I was on the
plane en route to California.
I remember my father riding a bike
with us throughout our village.
I remember roller-skating in the middle
of the street with my friends.
I remember never being able to find any
eggs during the Easter egg hunt!
I remember dancing in my sister's living
room and laughing out loud.
I remember holding my husband's hand
as we walked into the movie theater.

I remember the birth of my sons.
I remember watching my grandsons'
joy on rides at Coney Island.
I will always remember the pride I felt,
attending church with my dad!
I will always remember the happiness on
my mom's face each time my sisters
and I took her to Las Vegas for her birthday!

Common Courtesy

March 4, 1993

Father said, "Always respect your elders."
So we said, "Yes, sir," and, "Yes,
ma'am," to all adults we
came in contact with. Father and Mother warned us
that we would be dammed to hell otherwise.

As I got older, around eleven years
old, this behavior was
still expected. Saying good morning
to strangers just to
give them the time of day became absurd.

Yet upon my arrival to New York, I felt out of place,
using sir and ma'am after every yes or no. People
thought I had no pride in myself and
was weak. I later imagined that they
thought that I was some sort of indentured servant.

Inner-city education revealed a
truth unknown to me
because I had come from
Charleston, South Carolina.
I learned that if I said sir or ma'am,
no one would respect me.

How odd I felt for such a long time.
Well, I guess Dad didn't
know everything except what he was
taught. This particular family
and cultural custom was not passed
on by my siblings or me to our
children. But we do teach common courtesy.

Splendidly Slender

May 25, 2019

Splendidly slender in retirement
Is not always as simple as being able to pay the rent

But awakening each morning to
a wonderful new day,
Just appreciating the calmness
surrounding you, as you lay.

To peer out of the picture window
at a flowering bush,

The stained-glass disk gave it meaning.
The colors made me giggle
with a gush.

Being thankful for small charming things,
I don't wear jewelry, not even my wedding rings.

My eyes are wide open to life's simplicities,
Above all thoughts and gravities.

Watching the bluebirds await in the
trees while I feed the cats.
Then they swoop down when all is clear
and eat from the dishes on the mats.

Enjoying nature daily, which is
perfect and purposeful,
Understanding always that God is so merciful!

Touching My Hair

April 16, 2019

Why did you touch my hair?
What does it mean?
I have never thought about
Touching someone's hair!
For what?
I mean, for what purpose?
Are you serious?
What are you trying to tell me?
Do you have a problem?
Who invades someone's personal
space without permission?
Isn't that very personal?
I didn't see it coming!
Do my braids threaten you?
It's a hairstyle I've inherited from my foremothers.

I have worn it all of my life. So I guess it is a gift
from my ancestors. A cultural
style innately passed from
generation to generation, I have learned.
I don't touch anyone's hair. It's
rude and invades privacy!
So don't touch my hair! I don't know
where your hands have been!
Be respectful and thoughtful! Just
look and admire from afar!
Back up and keep moving!

Time

Dedicated to my brother-in-law Sean (Barr),
who we visit in Sing Sing, with love

March 28, 2019

When you're doing time, things get very corrupt.
The moment you walk in and a
cellmate says, "What's up?
They immediately want to know what you're in for
Then get right down to the logistics
and straight to the core.
Each morning you awake to a nightmare,
Now wishing you've never done it with a swear,
Waiting week after week for a visit from
a loved one with cash in tow,
Saying to yourself, "I'll never do
anything wrong anymore,"
Hoping someone would write, especially
since you have family galore…
Praying for a package of any kind,
Trying to stay focused and not lose your mind…
Repenting and setting goals for a life beyond,
Thankful to get letters from family
members and friends then rush to
Reply, always quick to respond!

Teaching

Dedicated to all the students I taught over a thirty-year career as an educator (1986–2016)—thank you!

May 13, 2019

Teaching allowed me to educate students
and permit them input without hesitation,
Assuring them that I had faith in their leadership for
the next generation…

Encouraging students to speak their minds
without procrastination…
Modeling how to use their prior knowledge as a tool
is always an effective motivation.

Witnessing young learners move
forward during graduation
was a proclamation.

Visions of 9-11

....

January 1, 2020

Something's going on!
There's been an accident at the World Trade Center.

With all the tourists in New York City,
it didn't really cause us a reaction,
so we kept working without any hindrance.

Teachers speculated it could have been a
sightseeing helicopter that flew too low.

We just focused on instructing, our regular flow.

I peered through the window at
the Manhattan skyline,
over the Jamaica Bay.

Then I saw one of the twin towers
going down to the ground,
disappearing like a flower getting
picked in the month of May.

Now observing one tower standing,
news came that we
were under attack.

Eventually, we learned that the
planes leaving Boston were
hijacked and never coming back.

Soon, the next tower was on fire and
fell quickly onto the ground.

Parents arrived to collect their children
early, making a desperate sound!

Transfixed and traumatized, we
listened sharply to the latest
news on a battery-operated radio.

We wondered how we would make it
home, when it was time to go.

The smell had already flowed over the water.

A huge barbeque scent of the burned
bodies I inhaled caused an
immediate mental and physical disorder.

Listening to the news of what exactly occurred.

Pictures of desperate people jumping
out of windows emerged.

For the rest of my life, I will never forget 9-11.

Always praying for the families'
strength and the spirit of the
victims, who have now gone on to heaven.

Appleton

February 19, 2020

On an ancient hilltop lies Appleton Estate.

Fields of sugarcane are flowing, fleecing the terrain.

Visitors' vibrant vigor in amazement
of the vast history

As the guide glances over the
large group gazing at the
historic artifacts glowingly.

Sampling, sipping the aged rum,
symbolic of the staple
heritage.

The pride of Jamaica forever!

About the Author

Mary Harris was born and raised in Charleston, South Carolina. She is the seventh of eleven children.

Her early education was earned in segregated poor schools. There, she was nurtured and taught leadership qualities, inspiring her to teach her younger siblings to read and write daily with conviction.

At age thirteen, she was transplanted and grew up in Rockaway, New York. Her AP high school English teacher called her "the edification of good things in small packages." This encouraged her to achieve all of her goals.

From that day on, she strived to become a teacher, majoring in English literature and minoring in education, and she achieved a BA degree from York College. While volunteering as a recording secretary for three years for the alumni association, she was awarded the Meritorious Service Award. With an eagerness, she worked two jobs while raising a family and attended Brooklyn College to earn a master's degree as a reading specialist for kindergarten to the twelfth grade. As an exceptional student, she was nominated and inducted into the International Honor Society of Education-Chapter Kappa Delta Pi. She then received a master's advanced degree in school/district administration and supervision. Mary served as an educator for thirty years.

Today, Mary is retired and living in Long Island, New York, with her loving husband, Travis. She has two adult sons (Travis and Kareen), four grandsons, two great-grandsons, and one great-granddaughter.